Leaving Santa Croce

Leaving Santa Croce

The History of
Maine Evergreen Nursery
and the
Costa Family in America, 1901-2008

C. Kay Larson with Russell P. Trocano

Copyright © 2008 Maine Evergreen Nursery, Inc.

All rights reserved. Any reproduction, copying, redistribution or transmittal of this book or any materials contained herein, in whole or in part, in any form or by any means now or hereafter known, electronic or mechanical, including photocopy, recording, or any information storage or retrieval system, is strictly prohibited without the prior express written permission of Maine Evergreen Nursery, Inc. Correspondence regarding permission to reprint all or any part of this book or any materials contained herein should be addressed to: Maine Evergreen Nursery, Inc.

ISBN 13 Softcover: 978-0-578-00580-5

Printed in the United States of America.

To order additional copies of this book contact:

Maine Evergreen Nursery, Inc.
203 West Pleasant Avenue
Maywood, New Jersey 07607
Ph: 201-843-6808
Fax: 201-843-8845

Russell P. Trocano & Associates
60 South Maple Avenue
Ridgewood, New Jersey 07450
Ph: 201-445-0777
Fax: 201-445-0669

Book cover design: C. Kay Larson.
Production manager: Catherine Wall.

Contents

Introduction 11
Chapter One: Hackensack: A Most Pleasant Village......................13
Chapter Two: Coming to America..23
Chapter Three: Maywood:
    A Place of Stylish Abodes and Ample Grounds. 39
Chapter Four: The Greening of Bergen County..............................52
Chapter Five: A Summer Camp 69
Epilogue: 74
Bibliography..76
About the Authors...78
About Maine Evergreen 79

List of Illustrations

Bust of Oratam, Lenni Lenape chief, by John Ettl. *History of Bergen County* by Frances A. J. Westervelt, Volume 1.

The "Green," Hackensack, New Jersey, nineteenth century. Westervelt, Volume 2.

European immigrants arriving on Ellis Island steamer, 1912. Library of Congress.

Rosenbloom textile mill, Paterson, New Jersey, 1942. National Archives.

English and citizenship class for Italian immigrants, ca. 1920, Newark, New Jersey YMCA. Library of Congress.

Italians were the first importers, distributors, and sellers of bananas, location unknown, ca. 1900. Library of Congress.

Main Street, Hackensack, New Jersey, ca. 1915. Westervelt, Volume 2.

Italian-American mother who had two sons in the army trims threads from American flag at Annin Company, Verona, New Jersey, 1943. Library of Congress.

Italian shoemaker who volunteered as air raid warden during World War II. Library of Congress.

Colonial Brinkerhoff house, Maywood, New Jersey. *History of Bergen County* by James M. Van Valen.

Dutch kitchen, Bergen County. *History of Bergen County*. Westervelt,

Illustrations *(cont'd)*

Volume 1.

Gustave L. Yaeger estate, ca. 1900. Van Valen.

Future President Gerald R. Ford, World War II veteran, his wife Betty and children posing as a typical affluent middle class family of the post-war era in the leafy backyard of their suburban home. Alexandria, Va. 1959. National Archives.

Tree planting by members of Federation of Women's Clubs, location unknown, May 1920. Library of Congress.

Early American nursery advertisement, *North Carolina Sentinel*, 9 January 1830. America's Historical Newspapers, 1690-1920. Electronic database: New York Public Library.

Park Avenue, New York, New York flower plantings provided by Julius Roehrs & Sons greenhouses, Bergen County, 1973. National Archives.

Christmas tree mart, New York, New York, ca. 1890. Detroit Publishing Co. Collection, Library of Congress.

Entrance to Finderne farm, last family farm in Somerville, New Jersey, 1974. National Archives.

Red pine tree plantings, Hayward nursery, 1939. National Archives.

Santa Barbara County, California, a source of many of the country's flower seeds, 1972. National Archives.

Two stages of growth of Scotch and Jack pine and Spruce seedlings, 1934. National Archives.

Bust of Oratam, Lenni Lenape chief, by John Ettl, *History of Bergen County* by Frances A. J. Westervelt, Volume 1

Introduction

In the Bergen County Historical Society resides a bust of a Native American chief. This stonework features a craggy visage, neck, and shoulders--the veritable perfection of one's image of an American sachem. This is Oratam, chief of the Achkincheshacky, the tribe after which the city of Hackensack, New Jersey was named. Two miles west of Hackensack lies Maywood, home of the Trocano/Costa families, owners of Maine Evergreen Nursery, Inc., a wholesale firm, the subjects of this work.

To properly relate the history of the families and their nursery business, let us first glimpse at the towns in which they settled, for the history of Hackensack/Maywood is not unrelated to the success of the Trocano/Costa families in America. The moral of our story is basically the proverbial one: you can take the boy out of the country, but you can't take the country out of the boy. So first we will return to Oratam, but will continue on to relate the tale of Salvatore "Sam" Costa who left Santa Croce, Sicily in 1901 to start a new life in America. We will see that in some ways, Oratam and Sam are linked: both men, or Oratam's ancestors, came from far away places originally and both carried on venerable traditions of their countries; both men were "hard," Oratam's bust literally and Sam's personality figuratively for it took a driven man to succeed against odds, even in the boom towns of New Jersey at the beginning of the twentieth century.

Chapter One

Hackensack: A Most Pleasant Village

ORATAM WAS A CHIEF OF A BRANCH of the Lenni Lenape Native American tribe that resided in eastern New Jersey when the first Dutch settlers arrived. Although their sizes are uncertain, the Turkey and Wolf branches were small, perhaps numbering only 2,000 or so members. The Lenni Lenapes bore a proud heritage. Their name means "original people." Tribal lore conveys that they were the first western migratory tribe to reach the Atlantic shores from the interior, sometime in the mists of history. So surrounding nations, such as the Iroquois, had always paid deference to them. The Europeans and Americans, however, never displayed much, eventually forcing them back west, as far as Wisconsin.

For whatever period of time the Achkinchesacky lived in the area, historical writers agreed that their lands were some of the most beautiful and romantic in all America. Bergen, the county, in which Hackensack is located, now is bordered by the New York State line to the north; Passaic and Essex Counties to the west and southwest, respectively; Hudson County on the southeast; and the Hudson River due east, although boundaries have changed over time.

The county is pierced by three rivers: the Hackensack that runs some thirty miles; the Passaic that descends eighty miles, sprouting bubbling brooks and creeks along the way; and Saddle River of about eight miles in length. Farmland was cupped between hills that rise several hundred feet in the west and the trap rock steppes of the Palisade bluffs that are 5-600 feet in height that line the Hudson River. Two geological features have marked the county's history: its red shale stone and clay set beneath sand and gravel.

Surely the first European explorers marveled at the sights of woods and creeks, brimming with wildlife, fowl, and fish, and the free-flowing, majestic waterways of the Hudson Valley. These sights must have evoked both awe and fear. Europe was already heavily populated, except in border areas like the Scottish Highlands, and monarchs strictly regulated land and waterway usage. The New World had none of these artificial barriers and the extent of expanse of the North American continent was unknown, as was its geography, native peoples, and wildlife.

Thus, in the employ of Francis I, uniter of France, Italian pilot Giovanni de Verrazano and crew were dispatched to America to discover a route to the East Indies. They sailed from Dieppe in December 1523. First arriving off the east coast, likely the Carolinas, they then ventured north, past Sandy Hook, through the narrow channel, and entered New York Bay in April 1524. In 1609, Henry Hudson, working for the Dutch East Indies Company with the same goal in mind, famously sailed his ship, *Half Moon*, up the Hudson River estuary, reaching Albany on September 19th. More exploring expeditions followed and reports sent back to Amsterdam encouraged the burgher government to form the Dutch West Indies Company in 1621. Merchants and settlers were sent out and the first New Jersey town, Fort Nassau (now Gloucester) was founded on the Delaware River. After Peter Minuit took over as director-general, he traded Manhattan Island for 60 guilders (ca. $ 24.00) in goods from local chiefs. By 1627 he had reinforced his settlements on the island, by abandoning those at Forts Nassau and Orange.

Yet still seeking to expand trade, in 1629 the Dutch States General established patroonships. Wealthy settlers were granted land along sixteen miles of navigable rivers, as well as feudal rights to hold court and be exempt from taxation for eight years. The first patroonship granted in Bergen County was to Michael Pauw who founded Pavonia in 1630. The patroon colonies were largely burned out by the natives, but settlers such as the Van Vlecks, Rudolphuses, Schuylers, Planks, Van Vorsts, and Bouts continued to arrive. Conflicts with the local tribes persisted which prompted Director-General Peter Stuyvesant to order colonists to locate in a close settlement which established the village of Bergen in 1658. The naming of the town is still a matter of dispute. Some believe it is named after the Norwegian city of Bergen, as there were a few original Norwegian settlers; others consider a Dutch town to be the namesake.

In 1664, the region changed political hands after a small English fleet of four frigates sailed into New York Bay, forcing Stuyvesant and forces to quickly surrender. English dominance was firmly established with the signing of the Peace of Breda that ended the second Anglo-Dutch War (1664-67). Local government was developed by John Lord Berkeley and Sir George Carteret, proprietors of a royal grant that extended between the 41 degree north latitude line on the Hudson to the northern most point of the Delaware River. The first English charter was granted Bergen village in 1668. Following Carteret's death, his widow, Elizabeth, was made executrix. She sold the charter to a consortium of Quakers, including William Penn, who was granted a new one in 1680. In 1682, Bergen County was established and was partly reorganized in 1693. At one point it was known as New Barbadoes. Comprising a narrow strip of land, not more than five or six miles in width, north-south; and twenty-five to thirty miles in length, east-west, its borders were the New York State line to the north; the Hudson River to the east; the Hackensack River to the West; and the corporation line to the south. After several years of contested rule with New York colony, the region came under British government rule in 1702, based on a recommendation by the Board of Trade to end proprietary colonies.

* * * * *

By the mid-eighteenth century, eastern New Jersey benefited from roads and ferries run from Hudson River ports. The first commissioner of highways was appointed in 1694. The Pavonia Ferry began in 1733. Others sailed out of Jersey City, Hoboken, Weehawken, etc. On July 3, 1812, the day after *Jersey*, one of two steam ferries, first plied the waters, a passenger exulted, "I crossed the Hudson River yesterday in a steamboat with my family in my carriage, without alighting therefrom, in fourteen minutes……" The first horsedrawn railroad in America ran in Bergen County. The Hackensack and New York Railroad began service in 1856. Thus, the steamboat and railroads dawned a new era for the people of New Jersey, assuring that they would become the bedroom communities of New York City, as well as its produce suppliers.

Over three centuries, Bergen County's Dutch, English, and Huguenot farmers turned it into a breadbasket for New York City, and its vegetable and fruit bin besides. Produce ran the gamut of a farmer's industriousness: rye and wheat grain, corn, a variety of vegetables, apples, ciders, vinegar, apple whiskey, pork and beef, all wended their way to the metropolis and surrounding towns. Home-industry goods such as flax and wool cloth, handmade furniture, cedar chests, and long clocks were made by skilled craftsmen and women. The clay created booming brickmaking and pottery businesses that produced red and yellow stone cooking wares, now cherished by collectors of Americana. Because of the many kilns in the area, farmers made brisk sales in cordwood.

Gradually during the nineteenth century Bergen County accumulated other marks of prosperity, community, and learning: two newspapers, an insurance company, fire companies, medical societies, new mills and bridges, more schools and churches.

* * * * *

This brings us to the township of Hackensack, Bergen County's judicial seat, where the Costa family first settled. Situated on the banks of the Hackensack River, in 1923, one historian rhapsodized that, as a place of residence, the town was "probably unsurpassed by any suburb." Its 200 acres afforded broad streets, full grounds, and an abundance of air and sunshine, all luxuries to busy New York businessmen and their families who had begun to migrate there.

The township was formed following the 1693 county realignment. Originally settled by six or eight Dutch families, as late as 1840, some still spoke the language. John Berry was the first patentee. The first building was the Dutch Reformed Church, constructed on land donated by Berry. The first house was built in 1715.

At the beginning of the American Revolution, the town comprised about thirty families. Although small, its citizens nevertheless had long-lasting memories of the war. Gen.-in-Chief George Washington's headquarters was located there during his retreat to the Delaware River in 1776. In an engagement near the old Red Mill, Gen. Aaron Burr drove Hessian troops from the region. Local militia faced down combined British and loyalist troops, the court house being burned in 1780.

Following the war the community prospered, largely due to its hard-working farm families, active shipping routes, and the construction of railroads and turnpikes, as well as the education of its young.

In 1844, authors John W. Barber and Henry Howe described:

> Hackensack is one of the most pleasant villages in the ate, stretching along through the meadows, on two main streets…. There are several elegant mansions in the town, and a great addition is made to its appearance by the cultivation of shade-trees and shrubbery. From a hill about a quarter of a mile west is a beautiful landscape, comprising the whole of the town with its neat white buildings, the Hackensack quietly meandering through fertile meadows, and in the distance the high hills bounding the Hudson.

The "Green," Hackensack, New Jersey, nineteenth century.
History of Bergen County, Frances Westervelt, Volume 2.

There are 5 large stores, besides several smaller ones, which do an extensive business with the surrounding country. Six vessels are constantly plying between here and New York; a considerable lumber trade is carried on, and large quantities of pine wood for steamboats are brought from Virginia. The town has many mechanics of almost every variety, and 4 taverns.... There are two academies and one female boarding school, and also a select grammar-school, where young men are prepared for college....

In the wake of the industrial wealth created during and after the Civil War, Bergen County, and Hackensack, took on the trappings of the modern world. In Bergen County, the first gas, then, electric lights were installed, the latter in 1895. In 1878, the county was reorganized into fifteen townships and boroughs, including Maywood. The first trolley began running to 130th Street in New York City. In 1869, the Hackensack Waterworks Company was established. And more and more New York City businessmen and their families moved to Hackensack that boasted "pleasant homes and beautiful abodes." Sports and community organizations abounded: the Oritani Field Club; a boat club; a post of the Grand Army of the Republic, Civil War veterans; the Foresters, Masons, Odd Fellows, Knights of Columbus, and other fraternal groups; the Woman's Club and Eastern Star; the Boy Scouts. By 1900, Bergen's population had grown from 36,786 in 1880 to 78,441, a 47 percent increase.

* * * * *

A 1906 *New York Times* real estate article touted Hackensack, population 12,000, as being one of the "most progressive" in New Jersey. The old Dutch had died out (not really) and the new "American element," largely composed of New York businessmen, was "used to all the conveniences of the city, [thus] the town has had to provide itself with the highest class of improvements." More building was going on than ever before in its history, one 50-acre estate just having been sold for development. Even at this early date, housing demand excelled supply. Hackensack grew from a population in 1870 of 8,039 to 17,607 in

1920. In 1920, there were 210,703 Bergen County residents out of more than 3 million in the state as a whole.

This vast expansion can only be understood by viewing what was going on in the country as a whole. America had become a world economic giant by 1900, and much of its industrial capacity lay in northern New Jersey, funded by New York banks. In 1900, there were more than 190,000 miles of roads in the United States, more than in the rest of the world combined. Commercial ship traffic on Lake Superior, the region that supplied the steel industry with iron ore, was greater than that going through the Suez Canal. Already, there were more than 1 million lines of telephone wire strung across the country. The value of industrial production stood at $ 13 billion, seven times that in 1860. By 1920, the increase in industrial production and shipping spawned by World War I added to these totals.

Unfortunately, the mainstream newspapers and histories written between 1880 and 1925 largely covered the activities only of "the American element," in Hackensack. Newly arrived immigrants were ignored, even though the foreign-born accounted for a significant portion of Hackensack's population in 1900.

As Bergen County entered the technological age, the third major flood of European immigration was coming to the United States, mostly through the Port of New York. Whole families, teenaged and adult males, couples, most of whom had been crowded into the steerage compartments of steamships, came down gangways at Ellis Island to be processed by government officials. Ethnic groups were both the same and different from ones that had entered prior to the Civil War. The British, Germans, Dutch, and Irish still came. But for the first time, the vast majority arrived from Eastern and Southern Europe: Italy, Greece, Austria-Hungary, Romania, Russia, Turkey, and other nations. Economic conditions had largely forced these people from their homelands and drawn them to America: a population explosion in Europe following the Napoleonic Wars that resulted in growing demands for food; commercialization of agriculture that forced small farmers off their lands; the growth of the factory system in America that demanded unskilled labor; the relatively cheap cost of trans-Atlantic transportation. Of Italian immigrants, 80 percent were poor farmers and craftsmen arriving from Sicily and southern Italy. By World War I, one quarter of the whole Italian population had immigrated, five hundred thousand in 1900 alone.

Mirroring this national trend, in 1900 Hackensack was a polyglot community with many ethnic groups living in close proximity to each other, boarding in private homes and boarding houses. There were: English, Scots, Swedes, Irish, Finns, Russians, Austrians, Dutch, Germans, and Italians. Many New Jersey citizens had immigrant German and Dutch parents.

European immigrants arriving on Ellis Island steamer, ca. 1912.
Library of Congress.

The poorest arrivals who shuffled off Ellis Island onto ferries moved into the tenements of Manhattan's Lower East Side and the South Bronx which came to be dominated by the Italians, Jews, Irish, and Germans. More affluent Germans and East Europeans and Irish domestic workers settled in the Upper East and West Sides that were just being built up. Italians also moved into East Harlem in the 116th Street area in Manhattan and the Arthur Avenue section of the Bronx. Going out of Manhattan and the Bronx, residential neighborhoods in Brooklyn and Queens afforded leafy refuges from crowded Manhattan, as did the cities and suburbs of New Jersey.

Yet the American immigration story was not one just of how much money a European had in his or her pockets. Most likely few persons sailed off across the Atlantic Ocean to a totally unknown land. Even Colonial stock populations had moved to welcoming areas. Quakers from Rhode Island joined Scottish Quaker groups in East Jersey after Scotland founded its colony of Perth Amboy.

Hackensack census records from 1900 are quite revealing. The new Dutch and German immigrants likely were drawn by the existing communities, as in America trans-Atlantic ties could last centuries. A few new Dutch farmers and florists arrived. The Germans, in good part, were skilled craftsmen, working in such occupations as machinist, printer, silversmith, plumber, pipe layer; they also were bakers, dry goods salesmen, watchmen, and ice men. Along with Austrians, Germans were employed at the local brick kilns and as carpenters. The occupation of "day laborer," likely an unskilled construction worker, was noted by Germans, Austrians, and Italians. Clearly the local building boom was in full swing, and more new immigrants arrived by the day to service it.

Chapter Two

Coming to America

Salvatore "Sam" Costa was the first member of his immediate family to immigrate from the small farm town of Santa Croce in the Ragusa region of Sicily to Hackensack in 1901. A good portion of the population of Santa Croce had already settled there by the time Sam arrived. The same families had resided in these small Italian villages for centuries. Thus, the majority of the populations were probably interrelated and so immigration became a family affair, or at least one of cousins.

Immigration in early America was largely based on religion. Thus the pattern was for the late-arriving Italian Catholic immigrants to settle near German areas. For instance, Wisconsin's German population attracted Italians to Milwaukee, Kenosha, and Madison. Most likely these Germans were also Catholic and Old Lutheran that retained much Catholic ritual. Northern Italy also borders Germany and has strong Austrian influences, as it shares its border, too. Since the Middle Ages, trade from Turkey and the Middle East has entered Europe through Italy, with routes going north to the Baltic nations via German ports. So a feeling of shared historical ties and trade seems to have imbued the relationship between the Italians and Germans. Of course during the twentieth century, the Germans and Italians allied during two World Wars.

Germans had first settled in western Bergen County as part of the Colonial Pennsylvania "Dutch" (Deutsch) population which put them in proximity to the real Dutch. These first Palatinate Germans arrived in the eighteenth century via London and Rotterdam, Holland. Arriving Mennonites were both Dutch and German. High-church factions of the Dutch Reformed Church resembled the German Old Lutheran ones.

Regardless of religious persuasion, the 1844 historians noted the number of mechanics in Hackensack and Germans added to those numbers. An 1850 map shows two to three German churches in a number of northern New Jersey counties. After the Civil War, Thomas Edison, of Montclair, New Jersey, and his partner German-born, Henry Villard, established the General Electric Corporation, with German financing.

Although the majority of Italian men who immigrated intended to earn money to send back home and later return, America was so appealing that by the 1930s thousands of wives had joined them. The Sicilian women usually followed their men to America, and may have found factory or temporary employment, but most were expected to stay home as housewives and mothers, once married, often helping out in family businesses. Girls lived with their parents until they married. At first, young immigrant men crowded in boarding houses throughout the New York region, many having to take unskilled work as described above. Boarding houses were extremely convenient for the men worked long hours and needed a cooked meal when they got off. In Hackensack, scores of young German, Austrian, and northern Italian women, and men, also were employed as skilled weavers in the silk mills located in Hackensack, Paterson, Jersey City, and other cities. An 1894 newspaper article noted a strike at the Hackensack Silk Mill, on May 22. The night before at a mass meeting of 100, mostly Italian strikers, the German weavers had been denounced for not going on the lines. At this time American silk mills were at the height of production, but were largely replaced during the 1930s and '40s by rayon and nylon manufacturers.

The continual population, housing, and factory growth in Hackensack provided varied, booming opportunities for all. Immigrants were happy to find families from their own towns who would make them feel less homesick. Prospects were bright for young, ambitious men like Sam Costa, at the turn of the twentieth century.

* * * * *

When seventeen-year-old Sam got off the Ellis Island ferry in New Jersey in 1901, he had not just fallen off the proverbial "turnip truck." Unlike other Italian young men, he already had experience, gained in his small Sicilian town. Like most, his family were farmers, but at a young age, Sam began to market other farmers' produce for them to larger towns and in town. When he arrived in Hackensack, lacking money to buy farm land, Sam started plying his marketing skills. Although at first he held down two jobs, during the day caddying at the Hackensack golf

Rosenbloom textile mill, Paterson, NJ, 1942. National Archives.

course and at night shoveling coal at the Waterworks Company, soon he earned enough money to buy a horse and wagon and began to sell produce.

The day Sam bought his first supply of fruit and vegetables was a big one for him. On his first day out, he put half his money in his pocket, drove his wagon over the Hudson River into Manhattan, rumbled on to the markets, and bought his produce. At this time, however, Sam's English was poor. After he crossed the Hudson on the way back home, he got lost and was unable to ask or understand directions. Hence, his produce perished under the broiling hot, midday sun. Undaunted, Sam finally arrived home, got his directions squared away, and drove his wagon into Manhattan again the next day, using the other half of his savings to buy a second load of fruit and vegetables. On this trip, he successfully made his way home and was able to sell his goods. He must have heaved a big sigh of relief. Over time, Sam did very well on his route, and within a few years he was able to rent a store with rooms in the back. Presently the Hackensack bakery is housed in this same building. From his horse and wagon days, Sam had built up a clientele who became his store customers. Neighborhood families also shopped at his market, although Costa did have a few competitors.

When Sam left Sicily, he had intentions to marry Rose Belluardo, also of Santa Croce. And so Rose arrived in America within two or three years and they were married at St. Francis Roman Catholic Church, located on the corner of Hudson and East Broadway in Hackensack. For sure, all their Santa Croce cousins attended. Rose worked in Sam's store part-time and found the time and wherewithal to raise five children: one boy, Carmen, the oldest, born on July 13, 1913, and four girls, although, tragically, one died as a teenager. The children attended the State Street elementary school and Hackensack public high school. Carmen started working on the wagon, helping on the route, at age eight or nine; later when their store opened, at ages ten or eleven, the girls began work at the counter.

English and citizenship class for Italian
immigrants, ca. 1920,
Newark, N. J. YMCA. Library of Congress.

Clearly Sam had a natural talent for business. By the early 1930s, the Costas were successful enough to be able to buy two 2-story buildings on Hudson Street. One building became the family market where they, again, sold fruits and vegetables. In it, Sam immediately consolidated his costs and expanded his sources of revenue. He and his family lived on the floor above. He rented sections of the store to his cousin, Angelo Vasile, who ran a small butcher concession and to Irving Wigod who rented space where he sold dairy and canned goods. He also rented out the second building, located across the street that had a bar on the ground floor, adding to his income. So Sam's expenses and income were housed under two roofs, which offset each other to a considerable degree.

As great-grandson, Russell Trocano, explains Sam's success, coming from poor, often remote, country towns which had histories of conflict with each other, greedy plantation owners, brigandage, and foreign invasion, the main goal of most Italian families was first survival, then success. This meant: only family members were truly trusted and heavily relied upon; the male members were responsible for protecting the family; at first hard work was valued more than education; the main goal was to become independent by making money. Economic independence meant freedom for these newly arrived Sicilians. Says Trocano, "That's what you were told to do: make money. When my father met a lawyer once, he asked him, 'But are you making money?'" So whole families worked together in businesses that were passed down through generations and which afforded elders security in their old age. As a result Italian neighborhoods remained largely in tact, long after other ethnic groups had moved out.

Strong alliances were cemented with those groups with whom the Italians had a shared history and culture: Germans into whose areas they moved and later Hispanics whom they hired, given the similarities of language and Mediterranean culture and shared religion. As a concrete example, at the turn of the twentieth century, Italian grocers were the first to sell bananas in urban areas for the importers and distributors were also Italians. Due to their linguistic ties, they quickly picked up the rudiments of Spanish and peddlers met the banana boats at New York docks which steamed in from Guatemala and Costa Rica. As Russell notes, however, when unpacking, workers had to beware of black widow spiders. Following in this tradition, to this day, New York City government purchases a significant portion of Guatemala's banana crop for its school lunch program.

In a certain way, every Italian family business became a small fiefdom, headed by the eldest male. This did not mean, however, that the women had no say. In Sicily, they signed parental consents for children to immigrate; and they invested money husbands sent home. In America, they raised large families and worked in the family business

Italians were the first importers, distributors, and sellers of bananas, location unknown, ca. 1900. Library of Congress.

as time permitted. Extended networks of aunts, uncles, and cousins socialized and were expected to help each other out when troubles came. Italian mothers were known for their personal warmth and good cooking. Coming from a different ethnic group, Edna Costa, Sam's daughter-in-law, about whom we shall read more later, had to learn Italian cooking from her brother-in-law's mother. Italian mothers might serve turkey on Thanksgiving and Christmas, but they also might have been up all night making lasagna.

Because a certain "us-against-the-world" mentality existed in these first generations, every family member was expected to work in the business from a young age. The produce business is a tough one, since perishable goods are bought and sold, with small margins of profit. One had to quickly perceive where and how sales could best be made and sometimes make quick decisions. Competitors had to be beaten out. You had to b sure you got to the wholesale markets early, before the best produce was picked over. You came to know your customers and suppliers. If necessary long distance truckers would drive thousands of miles in one stretch to get goods to the market quickly. You had to know on which firms you could rely.

So over the years, Sam, Rose, and family learned the lay of the produce business in the New York City region. Fruit and vegetables came from a variety of markets: the Paterson markets then located near Railway Avenue; at what is now the Manhattan 125th Street beef market; the Bronx Terminal; the Hunts Point Market in the southeast Bronx. There Sam could purchase at volume discounts. The Costas made connections with buyers in Florida and had railroad carloads of fruit shipped to Hackensack, in, say, three days. If Sam bought fifteen loads of oranges, he could corner the local market for the week and be able to sell virtually the whole stock. Chickens could be purchased in Hackensack, but family members traveled as far south as Maryland to haggle with farmers over the prices of chickens and eggs. Bergen County farmers grew celery and lettuce. The old Dutch farmers, the Wyckoffs and Van Ripers, still had their apple orchards, which existed into the 1990s. But normally Sam did not buy from them, for he would have had to make a commitment to purchase an estimated amount at harvest time, which he could not predict. It was better to comb the produce markets in the cities, also to get the cheapest prices.

Then there was the business of learning the tricks of the trade. To keep items fresh, in the days before refrigeration, the Costa men stocked their trucks and wagons with large ice blocks. They watched over their shelves and saw what sold well, how fast, and in what quantities. During the summer when fruit was in season, they shipped it in under-ripe and sold it as fresh as they could; during the later months, or as it began to over ripen, these items might be sold in crates or bushels, at cheaper prices, for canning for the winter. The Costas only varied from produce when they stocked Christmas trees, wreaths, and decorations during the holidays. They kept open bins of fruit and vegetables on the sidewalk, like in Italy, thus avoiding needless packaging and storage costs. Awnings could protect produce from the heat of the sun, and fast ripening, in the summer. Their Italian neighbors also wanted to pick and choose individual tomatoes, potatoes, melons, peaches, and other items they were buying. The produce didn't need to be perfect; bad parts can be cut away. Each family had a lot of mouths to feed and every penny and purchase counted. This Italian custom of having open street bins today persists in Manhattan and all over the New York-New Jersey region, in all neighborhoods, and has been adopted by the Koreans, New York City's current small grocers.

The Costas learned how to keep customers. Because they had a neighborhood store, they already knew people from church or the community. So many customers were first generation Italian, as well as family, who wanted and needed to shop where the owners spoke Italian. The children could speak English to others.

Italians were also known for being persuasive salesmen who were good at encouraging customers to patronize their stores. They told their customers prices were cheaper at their stores, and this was the truth overall.

As a family enterprise, the Costas gave personal service and could give children special treats and watch out for them in the neighborhood, as did all the mothers. If a customer asked for an item, they would order it special, or sell in smaller quantities for widows or small families. New York lawyer Maria Doti who grew up in an Italian family in Brooklyn remembers thinking as a child that the Anglo supermarkets were supposed to be superior because they were "modern." But she liked the "homeiness" of her local Italian grocery.

Even during the Depression Era, Sam found ways to increase sales. Prohibition was in effect until 1934, but like thousands of communities in America, liquor did not stop flowing in Hackensack.

Sam's basement wine press used muscatel grapes which were high in sugar content which produces more alcohol. But the Costas also used any type of grape they could get their hands on. Often, they let grapes ripen until their skins shrank and then crushed them; with less water content, the amount of sugar was relatively higher, which again, produced more alcohol.

Most people in town were known to imbibe, and for sure, customers were happy to have a trustworthy supplier, if they didn't produce their own wines. Since Hackensack was relatively small and affluent, and politically controlled by the Irish, organized crime was notably absent, members of which were active in extortion and bootlegging. The rich were frequenting speakeasies in New Jersey and New York City and being taken out by launches to floating bars, just outside U. S. coastal limits in the Atlantic, which thus, were out of legal reach of federal law enforcement.

In spite of Sam's driving ambition, everything was not always just business. When Sam moved into his Hudson Street store, he sold one of his horses. By that time, he had developed a good deal of affection for his old horse. As Sam later told it, he sold the horse to a local ice man. One day, the man overloaded the wagon and the horse pulled off the front of it, having strained against the weight. As a result the ice load fell on the horse, killing it. When Sam found out about his horse's death, he said if he'd known this would be his fate, he would never have sold him.

So life in America was good for aspiring Italian families, even if every member had to work long hours at sometimes tedious, back-breaking work, inventorying and shelving items and loading and unloading crates and barrels. Since the large majority of Italian immigrants started working in blue collar jobs, as dockworkers, in construction and factories, long hours were not unusual. In spite of this, they understood that America offered opportunities and a better, easier life than one had in Sicily. As one Irishman put it: "Tis a grand country where there are pipes with water coming out of the walls." Women

Main Street, Hackensack, New Jersey, ca. 1915. Westervelt, Volume 2

didn't look fifty years of age when they were thirty. In a Minneapolis river section where Italians replaced Swedes in the frame homes that housed brewery workers, one remembered, as a child, listening every night in his bed for the voice of one Italian worker. He got off his shift at about 9 P.M. Before going home, he would walk to the middle of the nearby foot bridge and, at the top of his lungs in a good Italian tenor, sing "God Bless America." You could set your watch by that man.

The Costa Market would eventually become the largest in Hackensack. Sam and Rose eventually bought a house in Maywood where they lived until 1971 when Sam died. During most of this time, however, Sam was buying up more properties for rental purposes, both in Hackensack and Maywood. Prior to his death, he held private mortgages on those he sold. Thus, Sam had progressed from being a grocery peddler to a real estate magnate. He was well on his way to becoming one of the richest men in the first ward of Hackensack. As grandson Russell Trocano explains, "My family taught me never to depend on others to make money for you. Don't rely on the price of stocks or interest rates. Use your money to buy things you can make money off of yourself: things to sell, rent, or lease."

Also by the 1930s, excepting new immigrants, other Italians in Hackensack had moved up the rungs of the economic ladder, although most not as successfully as Sam. They got out of the common day laborer jobs into ones as salesmen, store and office clerks, waiters, and workers in the silk and paper mills and chemical factories. More skilled workers included: tailors, shoemakers, bakers, machinists, plumbers, firemen, and merchants. Florists, greenhouses, and nurseries, including some with Dutch owners, catered to affluent home and estate owners.

* * * * *

During these same years, Carmen, the eldest Costa child, was attending Hackensack High School. At some point he earned a spot on the football team. Sam, however, made him quit: to Sam, it was a waste of time; he wanted his son working in his store for him. After Carmen graduated, he normally put in 100 hours per week, working in the store and hitting the markets in the mornings.

While in high school Carmen met Edna Grathwohl whose parents were German and Irish. He married her in 1933. Like his enterprising father, while driving to Niagara Falls on their honeymoon, Carmen visited local fruit and vegetable growers. On their return, he continued working for his father.

Carmen Costa also had saved his earnings. So in 1934, he and Edna were able to move into a custom-built, brick home on the corner of Willow and Lewis Streets, in the Fairmont section of Hackensack, only one of three Italian families in the neighborhood. When their only child, Barbara Ann, began school, a few teachers made comments about the "Italian" girl in class.

In December 1941, World War II erupted, following the Japanese bombing of the U. S. Navy base at Pearl Harbor in Hawaii. Four days later, German Chancellor Adolf Hitler declared war on the United States. Thereafter, life changed dramatically in America.

Italian-American mother who had two sons in the army trims threads from American flag at Annin Company, Verona, New Jersey, 1943. Library of Congress.

Carmen was twenty-eight years old at the time. He was eventually exempted from military service, largely due to his age and because he was a father. But he did his duty, donning a white helmet and arm band, serving in a Civil Defense job as a warden on the lookout for attacking planes, enforcing the blackout, and putting in fire prevention measures. During the war, millions of American men and women worked in war charities, civil defense, and paramilitary groups; toiled long hours in defense plants; participated in salvage drives; and endured rationing of food and gasoline.

During these years, Carmen also started his own business. In his hours off from working in his father's store, he was selling used cars and even a few pianos out of his house. During 4th of July celebrations, he hawked fireworks. In 1946, Sam sold the Hudson Street store to Joe Chooch—"Chooch" was a nickname, meaning "dumb" in Italian—as is well known, Italians have nicknames for everyone. Thus Carmen began to work full-time for himself, using his father's truck to sell produce to restaurants, as he had kept his father's accounts.

In 1948, Carmen finally bought a building on Main Street in Hackensack. Two narrow stores fronted the street and an elderly woman lived in the upstairs apartment (memories are that she was

Italian shoemaker who volunteered as air raid warden during World War II, 1942. Library of Congress.

always calling Carmen to come up and fix things—the woman was a pest); warehouse space in the back was used for storage. The second store was rented to a man named Walter Barlow. In Carmen's part, he had his grocery.

Like his father, Carmen Costa initially did well in the grocery business. He was able to keep many of his father's customers and new ones came in. By the postwar years, the Costas had been in Hackensack for nearly fifty years, were well known and some of the most prosperous merchants in town. Carmen was appointed to serve on the board of the local New Barbadoes Bank that oversaw lending for building loans and mortgages. Given that northern New Jersey and New York produced and shipped mammoth amounts of World War II materiél, as of 1944, this new prosperity began to show up as increased home sales. Hackensack began booming again, as hundreds of veterans returned home from Europe and the Pacific and married in droves. Americans were aware of the staggering casualties the war had reaped. And so couples had lots of children which added to the population, and thus the business base, of Hackensack.

On the surface, the postwar building boom in Bergen County made it seem like Carmen's grocery store would continue to do well through the 1950s. However, the population was changing and merchants were making businesses more convenient to the American car culture.

The reality was that Sam Costa had built his business on the basis of the immigrant community in Hackensack—a common culture and language and proximity had drawn fellow Italians to his store. By the 1950s, however, the Italians who had been born in the United States had gone through the Hackensack public school system which produced a cultural shift. This generation had learned English, and although most stayed in the same neighborhoods with their parents, some moved to nearby communities, as Carmen would do later. Moreover hometown veterans had traveled the country and the world. Having returned from

Europe, some saw they could capitalize on their heritage, set up more Italian restaurants that served home cooking, and bring in a more diverse clientele. Yet Carmen was still relying on an ethnic base of customers that was declining and new ones were not being added in great numbers.

As to the car culture, the first McDonald's quick service restaurant opened in 1940 and their first drive-ins started in the early 1960s. Others such as A&W Root Beer and Dairy Queen ice cream stands took off in popularity. Drive-in movies were all the rage. By the mid-1950s, millions of teenagers were cruising in convertibles, fashioned by General Motors designers in sleek, jet motifs that featured wrap-around windshields and flashy, chrome bumpers and detailing. As cities and suburban towns expanded via wider thoroughfares, the "California style" shopping centers were strung along them. People stopped going to downtowns which had only two-lane streets. Gas was cheap and people thought nothing of driving miles to shop or to go to a movie or a dance. So for the first time, Costa's grocery store was getting serious competition from a firm named Packard Bamburger. Packard Bamburger incorporated selling factors which would be recognized today: the owners took advantage of volume discounts and sold a greater variety of merchandise, in greater quantities, in separate stores, all located under one roof, at lower prices. Customers could drive in and park in the big lot, as opposed to having to search for spaces on cramped downtown streets. Packard Bamburger even produced their own brand of Scotch and sold other liquor under their store's name.

Carmen had to make new plans. He saw greater opportunities in the nursery business. So he leased the grocery to Sam Vasile and moved on.

Chapter Three

Maywood:

A place of stylish abodes and ample grounds

This gentle reader brings us to the period when Carmen Costa shifted from the produce to the wholesale nursery business. For a long time, he had had an interest in horticulture, even while he ran the grocery store. He would spend hours reading *American Nursery* magazine. And, as noted previously, when in the grocery business, he was selling trees and wreaths at Christmas time. Eventually a customer suggested he sell flowers year round, too. In the area, the same merchants typically sold trees, shrubbery, and flowers, Henry Hay greenhouses and Holland Acres, being two examples. So in 1961, Carmen established Maine Evergreen Nursery, Inc., first renting property from a man named Eddie Stagg who was in the business in Hasbrouck Heights on Route 17.

After two years, Carmen relocated to Maywood, a nearby community, which was still fairly rural at the time. Until the 1980s, he rented the building and property of the Maywood Power company, a lawnmower sales and service center. He also bought two houses and a lot opposite the Power Company. Then in the 1970s, Carmen convinced Vinnie Villano who owned an auto body shop next door to clear out a space where junked vehicles were stored, so he could lease it. For many years the firm also had use of an old trolley track bed that ran between the house lot and Maywood Power that legally was owned by the town.

By this time also, a new member had been added to the family who could help run the business. Carmen and Edna's daughter, Barbara Ann, met Russ Trocano, Sr. in high school in 1952. They were married in 1959. Eventually they had one child Russell. Russ, Sr. became the foreman of the nursery, supervising orders and shipments, and dealing with employees and customers. Carmen still managed the general operation.

Maywood was a particularly good area in which to go into the nursery business for it had inherited a long and interesting legacy from its first Dutch settlers. It possessed strong architectural and decorative traditions that fit perfectly with Carmen Costa's visions for his new business. So before we look at Carmen's business in detail, let's take a peak at Maywood's past.

*****

Maywood, New Jersey is situated two miles west of Hackensack. It is approximately one by one and three-quarters miles square. Like the rest of Bergen County, Maywood began as a community of largely Dutch, English, and Huguenot farmers. The first settlers were: Daniel Ackerman, John Romaine, John R. Oldis, Andrew Voorhis, James and David Berdan, Cornelius Van Saun, Henry and Martin Terhune.

Farms were passed down through the generations, until the end of the nineteenth century when Gustave L. Yaeger and Henry Lindemeyer bought large tracts to subdivide into lots. Jaeger bought out

Lindemeyer's interests, sold the lots, and a village was established. The first mayor was Clarence A. Breckinridge. Good roads, modern sewer and water works, and electric lighting were soon installed. Community organizations sprang up. Three volunteer fire companies were established. A grammar school to the eighth grade opened. Maywood's older students traveled the short distance to attend Hackensack High School.

On a night out, residents might go to a vaudeville performance or movie at the Lyric Theater in Hackensack. During the late 1920s and '30s, movie tickets were only about $ .10, so even children could attend. The lavish musicals of the Depression Era featured wealthy, uppercrust characters who could have come out of Maywood, or at least summered near by. In 1932, Maywood's New Art School of Music advertised its performances.

Meanwhile residents had to earn their livings. Maywood's main industries were six chemical and a few cloth companies, and an art tile manufacturing firm. Old flour mills turned into concrete factories. The New York and Susquehanna Railroad and the 130th Street trolley carried suburban fathers the sixteen miles into New York City and back each day. By 1940, tunnels had been built under the Hudson River and more trains were running to New Jersey's northern suburbs at faster speeds.

*****

As previously had occurred in Hackensack, the suburban housing boom soon swept over Maywood. In 1900, shortly before Sam Costa arrived in Hackensack, the population of Maywood was 536. In 1920, it stood at 1,618, a 300 percent increase in twenty years. Property values totaled $ 2 million, which measures $ 16 million by today's standards. This little square of land was fast becoming known as one of the finest residential communities in Bergen County, as well as a splendid site for a country home.

The most striking feature of Maywood, which is very pertinent to our story, was the fine architecture and grounds of houses in the area. Newspaper articles suggest that a few Dutch estates remained into the 1930s, such as that of the Terhunes. But rare wealth alone did not account for the area's attraction.

When the Dutch settled East Jersey in the seventeenth century, Holland was the leading nation in Europe in industry, trade, science, and fine and decorative arts, to say nothing of flowers. Still today, elegant stone houses, once owned by affluent burghers, march along the leafy, tree-lined canals of Amsterdam. Dutch Baroque painting was at its height. For the first time in history, the sale of paintings was market-driven which resulted in a collectors' mania. Masters such as Rembrandt, Rubens, Vermeer, van Ruisdael and Steen churned out oils that spoke to the daily lives of the people of this republic. Still lifes, landscapes, flower stills, and home and work scenes found eager buyers. Then during the two years of 1636 and '37, "*tulip*mania" struck Holland. This large Turkish wild flower's appeal drew from its rich, vibrant, sometimes flamed, coloring and delicate petals. Tulips impressed friends and neighbors in an age when possession of exotic plants from the New World and Middle East demonstrated personal sophistication. The craze spread from the upper classes down. Rich and poor alike invested in bulbs and land, hoping to make quick killings in the booming market, although prices crashed once over supply set in. Later botanical prints of tulips and other flowers were used by salesmen to ply their plant trade. Another booming part of the Dutch economy was the millions of decorative, earthenware tiles produced in Delft and other Dutch cities, inspired by Arab and Chinese trade. Bergen County's early pottery businesses may have included tile making; they would have found ready places in Dutch kitchens and on fireplaces. Maywood's previously mentioned Art Tile Company that produced tiles in French Art Nouveau designs was a descendant of this tradition.

As a result of this economic and decorative explosion, when the first Dutch patroons and merchants settled in Bergen County, their homes set the tone for future generations, of even middling farmers. Presumably by the time New Jersey Dutch settlements had been secured at the end of the seventeenth century, etchings, paintings, tiles, and tulips had made their way into homes and gardens. Houses comprised: excellent architecture using local materials, bountiful lawns, and landscaped public spaces. Moreover, the natural abundance found in the New World placed few limits on what commoners or towns could procure and copy. For the first time, in the seventeenth and eighteenth centuries, as European and American middle classes grew, economic thinkers perceived that a person did not labor just to survive. People increasingly demonstrated a desire to improve the quality of their lives, largely by copying upper class tastes. By the time of the American Revolution, the colonies had one of the largest middle classes in the world.

In Maywood, Colonial Dutch farmers lived in stylish abodes, of which there were many in the village. They were: constructed of local red stone cut into large blocks, using superior quality mortar; with white painted wood scroll work adorning porches; practical halved Dutch doors; deep window casings; finely paneled doors and woodwork; and

Dutch kitchen, Bergen County. *History of Bergen County* by Frances Westervelt, Volume 1

Colonial Brinkerhoff house, Maywood, New Jersey. *History of Bergen County* by James M. Van Valen

carved mantelpieces. The more prosperous also owned feather beds, carved furniture, pewterware, looking glasses. Unfortunately, today, only about 200 Colonial homes remain in all of Bergen County.

Due to its scenic location and rural setting; its tradition of architectural excellence, and nearness to New York City, by the end of the nineteenth century, a number of wealthy businessmen called Maywood and the surrounding Bergen area home. We have already mentioned Gustave L. Yaeger who besides owning the Maywood Land Company was an entrepreneur, having filed seventy patents for inventions. Ernst Bilhuber, an engineer, owned a steel wire works

Gustave L. Jaeger estate, ca. 1900. Van Valen.

company and served on the German national committee of the 1876 Centennial Exposition. The Colonial Brinkerhoff homestead he bought was known to have exquisite grounds. Edward D. Easton began his career as a local New Jersey reporter and became a stenographer for the U. S. Lighthouse Board in Washington. He and other stenographers took an early interest in the new "talking machines" or graphophones, since they mechanized their handiwork. Easton formed the international Columbia Phonograph Company, came back to Bergen County, and established a 50-acre estate in Arcola. An old Huguenot family, the Loziers, descended from artistic lineage in France. John built a 300-acre horse farm that was said to "surpass all others of its kind," in modern technologies and breeding. With this type of wealth and expansive home grounds in the area, the rich were bound to beautifully landscape their home lawns and the local "Joneses" would be trying to keep up with them to the extent possible.

The stock market crash of 1929 did little to stem the tide which flowed to New Jersey "garden suburbs" that by then included apartment buildings, rentals, and small homes. In April 1932, during the depth of the Depression, *The New York Times* reported fifteen new homes were under construction in Maywood. In September a headline announced: "Residence Sales Brisk in New Jersey." During the next few years, purchasers seeking bargains seemed to have bought foreclosed homes. By 1934, pent up demand began to drive the market. Edwin J. Murphy purchased a house and lot for $ 27,000, worth approximately $ 300,000 by today's measure; the sale was a typical one.

Finally by 1937, confidence pervaded the market. Although there were still takeovers by savings and loans, great interest was being shown in old homes. Buyers were renovating them with modern conveniences and reselling. Some of these renovations may have included the Dutch Colonial homes. In April 1940, fifty new "Country Club Estate" homes were slated for Maywood. By 1941, "new sales records" were proclaimed for northern New Jersey. But the onset of World War II plummeted housing sales and construction.

The war finally ended on V-J Day, August 14, 1945, when the Japanese emperor capitulated and the Allies declared victory. During the next year, military personnel were mustered out and came home, seeking the American dream of a close-knit family ensconced in their own home.

Nationwide, the return of sixteen million servicemen and women created a severe housing crisis. Five million new houses were needed immediately; approximately 50,000 people were living in Quonset huts, basically high-class shacks that formerly had been used as army barracks and offices. Developers responded. In 1944, housing starts that had been stagnant during the war stood at 114,000. By 1948, the number had risen to more than one million.

One returning veteran, a former Navy Seabee, was a New Yorker named William Levitt. When the war first broke out, he and his family had constructed war worker homes in Virginia. While stationed overseas, Levitt supervised construction teams that built "instant airfields" on Pacific islands. Most of the men in his Seabee unit had been in construction in civilian life. At night they would sit and discuss their day's work, figuring out ways to improve their techniques. When Levitt returned to the States, he was a master builder, used to working against crushing deadlines. He also held an option on a 1,000-acre tract of land in Hempstead, Long Island, New York.

Levitt determined he would build a new type of "instant," very affordable home for returning veterans and their families, using the knowledge and skills he had honed in the Pacific. First he decided that the basement had to be eliminated, as it was the most costly and difficult part to build; an asphalt slab replaced it. He organized his work force into twenty-seven gangs, each assigned one building task, in that way, allowing semiskilled laborers to be employed. The trucks and teams would move from lot to lot, dropping off supplies, laying slabs, and performing assigned tasks on each house. By July of 1948, Levitt's crews were building 148 houses a week, or 36 a day. His attractive 4-room Cape Cod home, garage, and small lot sold for $ 7,000; other models' prices ranged in that category. Soon other developers copied Levitt's methods. By 1955, 75 percent of the housing starts in the nation utilized Levitt's techniques which had changed the face of America. Between 1950 and 1980, 60 million people had moved to the shiny, new suburbs. And the majority had lawns that needed planting; new schools and hospitals, as well as roads, highways, and town centers did, too.

Bergen County developers followed Levitt's lead. At first more apartment buildings went up. But then came the ranch and split-level homes that marked the era, although they sold for somewhat higher prices in the affluent Hackensack area. In the fall of 1948, builders were pushing to complete 100 new Maywood homes so families could move in before the winter. They were selling for prices that went from $ 11,500 to $ 16,900. But in 1951, 65 new 4½ room ranch houses were being sold in Maywood for a mere $ 9,000, features of which included attics

Future President Gerald R. Ford, World War II veteran, his wife Betty and children posing as a typical affluent middle class family of the postwar era in the leafy backyard of their suburban home. Alexandria, Va. 1959. National Archives.

and cellars. Older homes were also sought. The new drive-in shopping centers dotted the area to meet the rise in population; they might include a bowling alley, restaurant, grocery, drugstore, and bakery.

In keeping with its natural scenic setting, decorative tradition, and affluent tastes, Maywood's developers and residents were very concerned with how their lawns and grounds looked. Since they first began to be built up just prior to the Civil War, American suburbs offered the prospect for homeowners of having the best of two worlds: access to the bright lights and cultural activities of the nearby city and a more "healthy," rural setting in which to raise children. Copying the pattern of the British landed aristocracy, suburban wives were supposed to live leisured lives, free from drudgery, with freedom to engage in favorite activities such as gardening. (All the new electric appliances would also help them rush through housework, which was really not part of the leisured image.) Thus, regardless of other circumstances, at least one bright spot had always existed in Bergen County residents' lives: their gardens and lawns.

By the 1930s virtually every town had its Woman's Club, a section of which was normally devoted to gardening. There were even men' garden clubs. Bergen County gardeners formed a federation of garden clubs. All over suburban New Jersey and New York, elaborate, weekend-long flower shows were held that featured such varied display and talk subjects as: rock gardens, Mexican gardens, floral arrangements, table decorations, nature trails, roadside plantings, and those on single flower categories such as giant zinnias and dahlias. The 1934 Bergen County show featured hundreds of displays. Winners included: F. Kurzenknabe of Hackensack in the "incurved cactus" category; Maywood's F. Berkhofer's "Basket of Twelve" display; Mrs. P. Risoli's gladioli, also of Maywood.

During World War II, as armies tramped over territory and local populations evacuated, food became a very scarce commodity worldwide. Following the World War I tradition, the Federal

Tree planting by members of Federation of Women's Clubs, location unknown, May 1920. Library of Congress.

Government began to urge every family, garden club, and employer to cultivate "Victory Gardens" to grow food. In 1943, the Bergen County planning board issued soil fertility maps to gardeners, so they could tell whether their plots were suitable for vegetables and if so, whether they needed fertilizer. Flower shows converted partly to garden shows that featured talks on such topics as: storing your vegetables after the harvest, canning, and children's and employees' gardens. The need for paper may have prompted some to grow or sell trees.

* * * * *

Thus by the beginning of the postwar period, Bergen County, and Maywood, in particular, had long established traditions of pride of place, led by the wealthiest New York and New Jersey businessmen and their leisured wives. Garden clubs are still active. After Carmen and Edna moved to Saddle River around 1970, she became president of the Saddle River Garden Club. A local landscapers' association was formed in Maywood.

    The building boom that had basically not ended since its start in the 1890s, had assured landscaping of private gardens, as well as those of businesses and government buildings and thoroughfares. So the prospects looked bright for Carmen Costa when he opened his fledgling nursery company in 1963.

Chapter Four

The Greening of Bergen County

When the Costa family switched from the grocery to the nursery business, they were entering a cherished American trade. Americans had long viewed the vast availability of trees and lumber as a God send. In Europe the monarchs were sovereign, not the people, which meant they owned the land. A tree shortage existed early on, making it illegal, at least in England, to chop down trees. When German Hessian soldiers marched with British Gen. John Burgoyne down the Hudson River Valley in 1777, they were scared to death. They had never seen, or been in, such thick, deep forests, and ones with very wild animals at that. On the Continent only the aristocracy owned vast hunting parks, so commoners could not provide for themselves, unless they poached. But in America, for the most part, restrictions on lumbering and hunting did not exist and land was basically free for the taking, at least until the courts caught up with you.

Colonial newspaper advertisements show that even prior to the American Revolution, farmers were cultivating large tracts of land that could comprise enormous orchards, numbering as many as 1,400 apple, pear, nectarine, peach, and cherry trees. Timber in "great abundance and variety" was sold for barrel staves, naval stores, and lumber. With greater urbanization and better transportation, nurseries began to appear by 1810. The Strawberry Hill Nursery of Greenwich, Connecticut advertised fruit, locust, and horse chestnut trees, as well as grape vines, flowers, and shrubs. In 1830, D. & C. Lambreth of North Carolina sold fruit trees that were only "really worthy of cultivation," as well as hardy, ornamental plants and those that needed "the protection of the parlor." During and after the Civil War, timber was in short supply and tree farming began, increasing in annual output after World War II with American businesses' worldwide expansion.

In Bergen County, Julius Roehrs established the Mammoth Flower Garden greenhouses in 1884. A German immigrant who had apprenticed at the Kiel Botanical Garden at the University of Holstein, Roehrs accepted a job supervising the orchid collection of M. Sieman of Jersey City in 1868. His own wholesale flower business eventually consisted of sixty buildings, covering fifteen acres, in which a variety of flowers were grown: orchids, tulips, lilies-of-the-valley, hyacinths, lilacs, and so on.

* * * * *

FRUIT TREES AND GARDEN SEEDS

D & C LANDRETH

Nursery & Seedsmen, Philadelphia

OFFER for sale an extensive and well selected assortment of FRUIT TREES, comprising the most celebrated and desirable varieties of

Apple, Peach, Pear, Plum, Cherry, Apricot, Nectarine, &c.

In making the selection of the kinds cultivated by them for sale, reference has been had in an especial manner, to the quality and time of ripening, so as to obtain a regular succession of good fruit, excluding all such as were not really worthy of cultivation; having carefully pursued this course, they offer the selection to the public with the fullest confidence.

The ORNAMENTAL DEPARTMENT is equally worthy of attention. The collection of beautiful plants both hardy and those which require the protection of the parlor, is not excelled in the Union. And the prices at which they are offered, far below those demanded at other establishments.

Priced Catalogues may be had *gratis* of the subscriber, by whom orders are received.

THOMAS WATSON

Early American nursery advertisement, *North Carolina Sentinel*, 9 January 1830. America's Historical Newspapers, 1690-1920. Electronic database, New York Public Library.

Park Avenue, New York City, flower plantings provided by Julius Roehrs & Sons greenhouses, Bergen County, 1973. National Archives.

Carmen Costa's initial foray into the sale of Christmas trees grew out of a literally hallowed European tradition. Ancient societies, worldwide, lived according to nature's seasonal cycles. Primitive peoples saw plants, trees, and landscapes change during the year, so it made sense that early farmers would believe spirits lived in them. In many societies, trees were used as sacred gathering places. To celebrate the Winter Solstice, Finnish Sami tribes put small bits of food in trees. Celtic Druids pinned apples to oaks. As Germany became Christianized, "Paradise Plays" featuring the Biblical story of the fall of Adam and Eve that predicted the arrival of a savior were put on in town squares before a "Paradisebaum" that was surrounded by lights and hung with apples and wafers cut into star, angel, heart, and bell shapes. After Queen Victoria ascended to the British throne, her German husband, Albert, brought the Christmas tree to England in the mid-nineteenth century. Although in New England, the Puritans had not extensively celebrated Christmas, by 1860, the great pre-Civil War German immigration helped spur the Christmas tree tradition. Queen Victoria's glittering Anglican family also served as a role model for Americans, as British-American ties remained strong, well into the twentieth century. American women controlled the "domestic sphere" and so ensured a pride of place. In a more prosperous, pluralistic, post-Civil War society, more cash and "store bought" goods were available, and more elaborate Christmas traditions began to be celebrated. The tradition of the Christmas tree is one that has changed relatively little over time.

Thus, Maine Evergreen wholesale nursery began for the same reasons those in the early nineteenth century had: owners catered to an increasing urban population where a building boom was occurring and it was too expensive for contractors, landscapers, and garden centers to buy directly from growers who could be located anywhere in the country. In the mammoth post-World War II construction spate, more farms and estates in northern New Jersey were turned into housing developments; shopping centers; government office and business complexes; and county, state, and federal highways, all of which needed landscaping.

Christmas tree mart, New York City, ca. 1890. Library of Congress.

Entrance to Finderne farm, last family farm in Somerville, New Jersey, 1974. National Archives.

As in any enterprise, when he entered the nursery business, Carmen first had to learn it, by trial, error, and experience. One has to know one's customers. One has to decide into what part of the market one's product is going to fit: should you try to suit the general buyer, or focus, in whole or part, on a segment and fill the needs of niche buyers. These decisions can be tricky. If one tries to attract the general customer, one could have lots of competition. But if one tries to succeed only by filling the needs of niche buyers, would there be enough of them to allow one to make a profit?

Other questions arise. Fundamentally, regardless of the market segment, one must ask, what are customers looking for: what types of trees and shrubbery just look good; what is popular; what types of greens and flowers do they want for their gardens vs. their driveways and walks; which ones suit the soil of the area; to what kinds of diseases are different plants prone; what pests do they attract and how difficult are they to get rid of; how much maintenance do they need; does the average resident want to spend time working in his or her garden and really learn about plants? As an example of the above, hydrangeas are perfectly attractive bushes that bloom pretty pink and blue flowers. But if there is not enough acid in the soil, the flowers turn white, which gives them a slightly weedy appearance. As another, one type of evergreen shrub is "taxus." In years past, they have been quite popular, but currently customers want other kinds, largely because the local deer eat them, thanks to the recent explosion of the deer population in New Jersey. Needless to say, this information curve was filled in over time for Carmen by the landscapers and greenhouse owners who were hearing directly from their retail customers. Sometimes, what was bought depended upon whether residents had paid caretakers. So in order to get sales, one had to understand the needs of the buyers who were the professionals. Over time, Carmen got answers to all these questions.

Carmen started with the basics to sell to florists, garden centers, landscapers, and cemeteries. He purchased Christmas trees, in multi-tree bundles from Nova Scotia, as well as plantation and natural trees sourced from Maine, Quebec, and New Brunswick. In addition, Maine Evergreen carried a full line of Christmas greens, including wreaths, roping, brush, and grave blankets. Smaller items comprised florist wire and picks, pine cones, plastic decorations, and ribbon to go on them.

As to a market, in Maywood residents bought within a fairly small range of: shrubbery, flowering and deciduous trees, fruit trees, and flowering bushes. So Costa aimed for standard items, selling quality: evergreen shrubs, junipers, yews, boxwood, ilex, taxus, barberry, and holly trees; linden and magnolia flowering trees; maples and ash for colored leaves; rhododendron, forsythia, lilac, azalea, and hydrangea flowering bushes; apple, pear, and cherry fruit trees and later ornamental fruit trees that bloomed, but did not fruit; in July and August, cacti were on the market. Exotic species such as Japanese maples or Ginko trees might eventually be sold, but only after they had become common.

For every new shrubbery item sold, the Costas had to learn about it. As an example, for their government buyers, they learned that sycamore and London plane trees survive New York City smog well. Maine Evergreen has sold thousands of trees and plants to the New York City Parks Department. Fortunately, Carmen's wife, Edna, worked as the firm's bookkeeper and payroll administrator. She was also a good gardener. Often when a customer would ask what to buy or how to plant an item, Carmen would refer him to Edna who would take time to discuss plans with landscapers and contractors.

By the time Carmen opened his nursery business, he already knew many of the landscapers, florists, and retailers in the area, from having lived and worked in the community for so long. These buyers were best off relying on a knowledgeable wholesaler who could ship in and sell them quality trees and plants at reasonable prices. As an example construction deadlines were normally tight, so contractors couldn't have their men wasting time driving around shopping for shrubbery, the planting of which was a very small part of their work. Moreover, relatively speaking, the shipping costs were prohibitive. Over time, as he had done in the grocery business, Carmen built up his business by establishing and maintaining relationships, which succeeded in keeping customers and attracting new ones through referrals.

Maine Evergreen long-time employees also curried relationships and provided a sense of continuity. Both Guillermo "Gil" Gutierrez and Tony Dones came from rural backgrounds.

Gutierrez grew up on his father's large farm near Puebla, Mexico where they grew corn and watermelons. He was only able to go to school for short times during the year, but wanted to go to college. One of his dreams, as a youth, was to buy a Ford Mustang, a model that was extremely popular with teenagers in the 1960s. So Gutierrez saw his best opportunity as immigrating to the United States, getting a college degree, earning money, and returning home. When he first arrived in New Jersey around 1970, he worked for a short time in a nearby plastics factory. But a friend had started at Maine Evergreen and told him work could be found there. Having grown up on a farm, Gutierrez liked working with plants again, and never moved back to Mexico. He married and raised his family in Paterson. His daughter got her college degree in accounting and is the one who now drives a Mustang. When Gutierrez first started, he did every job: loading and unloading the trucks, driving, stacking plants, cleaning up. During the early days, his wife would bring lunch for the workers on Saturdays. The men would sit under the trees in the yard and eat together. Gutierrez is now one of the most experienced employees at the nursery.

Tony Dones's story is similar. His family's farm was located outside Ponce, Puerto Rico. He has been with the Costa family since the mid-1950s, having started when a friend who was working at the nursery asked him to give him a lift to his job. Dones was in the navy at the time. This continued until one day, Carmen asked if Dones could help unload a trailer. After he was discharged from the service and returned home, he got a call from Carmen, asking him to come in to work for him.

As in other cultures where the spoken word was very important, way past the time written contracts were the norm, in their business dealings, men like Carmen Costa depended upon other men's sense of honor. You had to be as good as your word. As grandson Russell Trocano tells it:

> A lot of landscapers and greenhouse owners in this area became rich because of my grandfather. He always said, 'You can't eat alone.' He extended a lot of people credit during the planting season, debts which they would pay back when their jobs were done. At the same time, my grandfather always kept track. If a customer didn't repay what he owed or bought from a competitor, my grandfather cut him off. In poor societies where, Sam, his father came from, people had to depend upon each other; otherwise, they starved. Today's American urban middle classes don't understand this kind of group loyalty.

Gutierrez echoed these sentiments:

> Carmen also gave help and advice. He told landscapers what to plant, how to plant. He advised them about how to get started. He would schedule their payments. Sometimes men would come in here with only one or two dollars in their pockets. Carmen would give them advice and then say, 'OK, go out and find work.'

According to Trocano and Gutierrez, Maine Evergreen managers still run this business the old fashioned way:

> We rely on the relationships we've built up with our customers over the years. The secret is: If you treat your customers right, they'll keep coming back. A lot of them say to me, 'Gil, when you're here, we come here.'

There's also an art to selling. You need to know what prices to charge and for what. Some customers are only looking for bargains. Depending upon demand customers might only be willing to pay a standard price, even if a plant is a larger size. You have to have a sense of how much time to spend with each customer, who you can get a sale from, who's a waste of time.

You have to know your buyers' needs and sometimes tell him how he can use things in a different way. When we first started, a whole gang of us would often work on Sundays, helping landscapers plant, just to learn their business, so we could know how to supply them. For instance, commercial properties don't need fancy shrubs and trees, so you can sell cheaper items to those contractors. We never complained about the extra work—each job put an extra $ 1- or $ 200 in our pockets.

Carmen also understood it was important to function as part of the community. He established relationships with the fire houses, the policemen, the Boy Scout troops, some of whom bought in bulk for the holidays, sometimes to decorate their houses, other times to raise money for their charities. Commonly police officers moonlit as small landscapers and planters for construction outfits. One December day, Pat Reynolds, a future police chief, came in with a former convict who had just been released from prison, and so had little money with which to celebrate the holidays. Carmen dragged out about ten scraggly balsams and gave the best one to the man—along with a couple of dollars. Former convicts were not the only ones who could be desperate around holiday time. Carmen got a call one day from his driver: he and the workers needed help; they were on the way to the Bronx Terminal Market with a load of Christmas trees and thieves had tried to jump in the back of the truck; they needed reinforcements to help guard their load."

* * * * *

As the years went by, one of the biggest changes at Maine Evergreen was mechanization, mainly of loading and unloading of the trucks. Explains Gutierrez "When I first started working here, you wouldn't believe how busy we were." Of course, this was when Maywood, and Bergen County, in general, was still greatly expanding. "Six days a week, we'd bring seven to nine tractor trailers into our yard, with some backed up on the street. Just one trailer could contain, maybe, fifteen to twenty thousand plants, mostly in one gallon pots. We'd have to stack and count them, too." In the early days, there would be four or five of the grower's men in the truck who would push plants forward down wooden planks. They might use a hand truck or pick up half a dozen plants by their tops in two hands. This was a lot of bending and lifting, even if the plants weren't heavy. On average twenty-five men would work on big loads. Beginning in the 1970s, trucks with power tail gates started being used. The nursery acquired tractors and fork lifts. For instance, sixty-five bags are contained in one pallet of mulching material that can be loaded onto a lift.

In their new business, the Costas also had to establish connections with growers across the nation, as well as in Canada, and learn those business angles. Still a key to the business is to stock only those plants that grow in cold weather at least part of the year and have been acclimated to it. A Southern tree, like a magnolia, might be able to survive in a center avenue mall in New York City, because of the warmer microclimate created by sun-baked concrete and car exhaust, but a homeowner would have to grow it in a protected area. Only cut branches, wreaths, and mulch can be brought down from Quebec and Nova Scotia. U. S. Department of Agriculture regulations forbid trees with soil from being introduced for fear of disease and insects that might infest the soil. Large cut trees were normally shipped on flatbed trucks covered with canvas and wetted down so they wouldn't dry out. Plants shipped in "hot" or unrefrigerated trucks would survive only about ten hours. So Carmen and company sought out growers who were not more than one day's travel away. Mostly they were located:

Red pine tree plantings, Hayward Nursery, 1939.
National Archives.

on the Eastern Shore of Maryland, and in Delaware, Connecticut, and upstate New York. Maine and the Carolinas were basically the northern and southern shipping limits. Shipping costs were actually cheaper from the West Coast than the Midwest, because the latter area is more likely to have more freight demand. But if trees or plants were shipped from the West Coast, refrigeration was required. If one was willing to pay a premium, an Oregon trucker might be willing to haul products through in three days or so, driving about sixteen hours a day. This, of course, was before the Interstate Commerce Commission started cracking down on drivers' trip logs.

As Russell Trocano further explains the grower relationship: "You have to judge your suppliers' capabilities relative to your needs." For instance, a certain shrub might have been declining in use over the past years. A supplier in the South might only supply that single item and won't ship anything else in a truck load. In that case, "If we're

Santa Barbara County, California, a source of many of the country's flower seeds, 1972. National Archives.

overstocked, we're going to tell the guy to cancel our yearly order. We'll find a grower who can ship us two items, both of which we know we can sell that year."

Going into the 1980s, the business had to adjust to external events and conditions. During the OPEC gas crisis of the mid-1970s when prices skyrocketed, Carmen's trucks were pulled into their local gas station at night to get filled up, so the drivers didn't have to wait on the long lines during the day. As the 1-income family became rarer and the feminist movement got underway, more suburban women went to work. This left them less leisure time to do lawn work and participate in garden clubs. During the 1950s and '60s, it had not been uncommon to see housewives on their hands and knees, in housedresses yet, pulling up crab grass from their lawns, which they were determined to look perfect. Homeowners became less knowledgeable about what they were buying. Previously many had been near professional horticulturalists. Also more middle class families paid workers to do lawn work; it was not just the rich anymore who acquired this service.

As American businesses expanded nationally and internationally from the 1950s on, corporate executives relocated to the new suburban and exurban developments. By the 1980s and '90s, they might no longer live in one community throughout their business careers. Thus, although affluent homeowners might pay lawn and garden workers, because they did not view their homes as long term commitments, they might not invest in extensive landscaping, even if they could afford it. On the other hand, the same executive might demand an "instant" landscape for which he might be willing to pay a premium price. In that case larger trees might be recommended. But regardless of other factors, landscaping is very sensitive to the economy. When the economy is good, homeowners will consider hiring a landscaper, some of whom might have arcane specialties, such as in Oriental gardens. During the severe economic downturn of the early 1990s, the construction, architectural, and landscaping businesses suffered greatly. On the other hand, in the late 1990s, gardening rebounded as a national past time, perhaps due to the aging of the baby boom generation, even greater suburban sprawl, a reaction to being too tied to televisions and computers, and/or blackberry burnout.

Meanwhile great changes also took place in shipping. Containerization transformed the method and costs of truck and rail shipping. Starting in the late 1960s, suppliers began to grow their trees and shrubbery in cans, instead of them being field-grown, root-pruned, dug out, and balled and burlapped. Moreover, a variety of trees and shrubbery can be grown in pots. More container-grown than balled and burlapped (B&B) items can be loaded onto trucks because the containers can be stacked more effectively. Formerly nursery stock was available in flats; cups; one-, two-, three-, and five-gallon cans, as well as bushels. Currently material is also available in seven-, ten-, and fifteen-gallon cans. Another advantage is that potted plants can be installed more efficiently in the landscape because less effort is required than with B&B material. Thus buyers find them more desirable because they can be more easily transported and preserved. Potting, therefore, proved revolutionary in the green industry, as growers could ship in greater volume, with greater efficiency and wholesalers could purchase from more geographically diverse sources and preserve the material in better condition for longer perods of time. In turn, the retail garden centers and landscapers benefited from easier planting techniques that could then be employed by the landscapers and members of the public who purchased these products. Largely due to the 1956 Federal Highway Act, thousands of miles of new interstate highways were being built, making continental shipping of these containers safer and faster.

* * * * *

Aside from all the business factors, the men at Maine Evergreen had to learn about the plants they were selling. As Gutierrez tells it, when he first arrived, he didn't know a rhododendron from a tulip poplar, either in English or Latin (both names must be learned, as well as their subspecies). For instance shrubbery that grows well in shade include: boxwood, andromeda, ilex, and Manhattan. Customers respond to trends and, at least a few, are always looking for something different—enough with all the white and red impatiens! Juniper trees were "in" a few years ago, but are not currently, as with magnolias. Hydrangeas had fallen out of favor, but are now increasing in sales. Those brightly colored azaleas never seem to fade from popularity, but they have to be gotten ready at the right time for a Northern climate, not before mid-April. Southern growers need to be given advance notice, too, as to approximately how many will be ordered in the spring. New, genetically-engineered plants are constantly being developed, as are hybrids. A few years ago, only junipers were used for topiary. Today Bonsai junipers, blue spruce, pine, and Oriental pom poms are all in use.

BEAL NURSERY STOCK

Two stages of growth of Scotch and Jack pine and Spruce seedlings, 1934. National Archives.

Then there is the soil issue. Landscapers have to tell the wholesalers what type of soil a customer has and, generally, describe its water supply. If the soil is not very fertile, such as that that consists of clay or gravely dirt, it can be mixed with peat moss. In some cases, however, it will have to be dug out and replaced with potting soil, which can also be mixed with peat moss, which cuts the cost. Customers need to tell the Evergreen Maine sellers what the drainage in a yard is like: will a strong rainstorm wash everything away because of sloping ground that has no ground cover or tree roots to absorb the water, or are there areas that pool? As Gutierrez says, even though Bergen County generally has a certain type of soil, every lawn or grounds is different, and spots on them can be different. You rely on your customers to know that and to describe it to you.

Chapter Five

A Summer Camp

Beyond the business factors that changed over time, Maine Evergreen employees and customers did, too. Many stayed on however, for many years, which is a tribute to the company. Says Gutierrez: "I've stayed on because I liked the work and Mr. and Mrs. Costa and their family were very good to me."

With the above said, Maine Evergreen employees were a colorful lot, stemming in good part from the fact that the nursery was an all-male environment in which the work loads were demanding. The work force changed, as much manual labor was involved and shipments varied. Hence, Carmen had a bunch of tough guys working for him, in a few cases, former convicts and delinquents who needed work and whom no one else would hire. As a result, strong memories of the men and their idiosyncracies were retained.

There was the day a confused stag ran into the yard. Afterward, "Louie" bragged proudly about how he had "bulldogged" the deer to the ground and held him down till local animal control officers arrived. "Big Mike" was a former steel worker who only worked two or three days at a time, but showed great strength in lifting trees and pots. Some of the heaviest items were bales of frozen peat moss. A different Mike was found to be growing marijuana in the back of the lot. "Hector" jumped bail on a crime, went out to Chicago, but showed back up again for work a few years later. Russell Trocano remembers well the day "Johnny" accidentally stabbed a neighborhood boy whose father had to be held back from seeking revenge. Carmen had to keep "Bobby" somewhat out of sight of customers, as he was missing his front teeth. "Henry" was a little odd; although he dressed well, he always wore hush puppy shoes, which earned him the nickname "Shuffle Foot." One young fellow was a Goth cultist who sported black-painted fingernails; he didn't last long.

Occasionally men would bring with them neuroses from their native countries. "Pedro" had been born in Colombia and was deathly afraid of snakes, due to the number of poisonous ones in his country. This fear morphed into an extreme paranoia exhibited toward even little earthworms. As a joke, one day someone slipped some worms into "Pedro's" pants pockets. When he was getting off work, "Pedro" reached in to take out bus fare and immediately felt the squirmy, little devils. Nearly hysterical, he ripped off his pants and ended up standing in the yard in his boxer shorts screaming.

As had been the historical pattern, Carmen started out hiring other Italians and Hispanics, again relying on the ties of Latin culture. But many African-Americans worked for them, too. They valued anyone who put in a good day's work. Says Russell:

> Depending upon how many orders and shipments we had, sometimes there were twenty-five to thirty men working here. It was like a summer camp, with all these rough, young guys cavorting around, teasing each other, performing practical jokes, and sometimes getting into arguments. But most of them were good workers. And there were days when we worked from 6:00 A.M. until 10 or so at night. But my grand dad was the toughest of them all and kept them in line.

Gutierrez recalls that the biggest problem with the men was often not their personalities, but their sense of order which could be extremely lacking:

> They sometimes just don't 'get it' that pots have to always be lined up properly. You have to keep from having gaps in the line of pots. Customers will immediately know that the best ones have already been sold, if they see holes in the line. So it's a constant battle, even now, to keep all the plants and pots in the right order and to get the men to understand that this small act is important.

By the early 1970s, grandson Russell also began working in the nursery during the summers, at about age thirteen. Mostly he helped load and unload the trucks and deliver goods. He could work his own angles:

> I figured, they were getting my hours on the cheap, so I looked for the easiest way to work. I always offered to go on the long delivery hauls, say, a 3-hour trip to Long Island. That way I could sit and view nice scenery there and back, for about six hours. When we arrived, we often had thousands of pots to unload. The greenhouse owners would send out the counter girls to help, because they didn't want to waste a more valuable employee. Some girls who were tomboys would help lift the bigger pots, but if they were unreliable, we ended up doing most of the unloading.

As teenaged boys are prone to do, on a few occasions, Russell and friends just goofed off: spent an afternoon at a boardwalk arcade or took a swim in a private beach. Yet over the years Russell learned the business as well as his father had, and, having inherited Sam's gregariousness, established good relationships with salesmen, growers, and contractors across the country and in Canada.

Besides all the physical labor, there were social times, too. One worker, Jerry, would go deer hunting every year and usually bag a buck. So Carmen's cousin, Angelo, the butcher, would dress it and cut up the venison. Normally an employee dinner would be held to feast on it. At Christmas time, the trees would be almost all gone by December 15, although some might later be sold to the local Greeks who celebrated Epiphany. Yet this schedule freed the workers to celebrate Christmas on time. Mrs. Costa usually gave out shirts as presents and there would be a company party.

Recently, George Krayniak, who formerly ran his own landscaping business, has joined Maine Evergreen. The change he has noticed the most has been the type and quality of the worker. Often the new, young American workers are spoiled and don't want to work. They also have less respect for their elders, a complaint of every generation it seems.

*****

In spite of all these business changes, a substantial portion of Maine Evergreen's customer base has never changed. Approximately 20 percent of contractors and greenhouse owners are the same ones with whom the company has been dealing since the 1960s, AU Florist and D&D Landscaping being two examples. In the case of AU, they bought trees, wreaths, flowers, and peat moss from Carmen when he owned the Main Street grocery store. In some cases, Carmen and the owners had gone to school together.

Howard Kruse was a long-time landscaper who performed some of the finer work in Bergen County's northwestern suburban communities such as Franklin Lakes. He always wore a fedora hat, indeed so often that one day, Barbara Trocano saw him in the local Sears store without it and did not recognize him. He would roll into Maine Evergreen in his Ford pickup truck that he had decorated with metal lattice work on the sides. Says Russell Trocano:

Howard and my grandfather were great friends. He was in our yard almost every day, inspecting trees and shrubbery and conferring with my grandfather and father. As a matter of fact, he was one of the ones who assisted me in learning how to identify the nursery stock. He had such a keen eye that he could tell which grower a planting came from by its growth pattern. Howard was also the best in the business; he did the designs and jobs for *la crème de la crème* in this county. He was still working when he was well into his eighties. Unfortunately he passed away within the past few years.

Epilogue

Over the years, the physical grounds of Maine Evergreen have not changed dramatically. The 2.9 acres continue to be striped with rows of plants, flowers, shrubs, and trees, all in order. The big tractors chug in and out of the driveway. The small office exudes informality and a sense of friendliness and controlled chaos. But the surrounding area is more crowded than it used to be; houses are cramped next to the grounds; the Port Authority bus stops on the corner. So today Maine Evergreen exists as something of a rural oasis, tucked away on a cozy suburban street.

In the last few years, the largest changes that the company has seen have taken place. In 1997, Carmen Costa, the owner who established Maine Evergreen, died at age eighty-four. Like many folk who are tied to the soil, he worked until the week just prior to his death. As has been noted in the previous pages, Carmen was well known and liked in the community, particularly among his customers and former employees. Gutierrez said: "There were *a lot* of flowers at Carmen's funeral." In 2007, Russ Trocano, Sr., Carmen's son-in-law, retired and grandson Russell took over as general manager.

The company currently consists of five employees, besides Mrs. Edna Costa, the co-founder: Russell Trocano, the general manager, and longtime specialists, Guillermo Gutierrez, Tony Dones, Guillermo "Simitri" Delgado, as well as George Krayniak. With this group, over the years, Carmen Costa established an extended family that probably will not change much in the future. The heyday of suburban expansion has passed, but area businesses and families will come and go, and Maine Evergreen will cater to their needs. Says Russell Trocano:

> Only about 15 percent of family-owned businesses survive past the second generation. We're on to our fourth generation as a business family, so Maine Evergreen is an exception in terms of success. In the case of many family-owned businesses, the enterprises are not successfully passed down through the generations. In some instances, the business must expand or it will suffer. In other cases successive generations cease to be self-employed and in addition may very well enter other lines of work. Maine Evergreen looks forward to the future and even greater success, as it cooperates with suppliers and customers, as the green industry adapts and evolves, continuing on into the twenty-first century.

BIBLIOGRAPHY

Books and Periodicals

Brettell, Caroline B., reviewer of Linda Reeder's "Widows in White: Migration and the Transformation of Rural Italian Women, Sicily, 1880-1920," *Journal of Social History*, Vol. 38 no. 3 (Spring 2005):800-12.

Clayton, W. Woodford. *History of Bergen and Passaic Counties, New Jersey, with biographical sketches of many of its pioneers and prominent men*. With William Nelson. Phila.: Everts & Peck, 1882.

Goodwin, Doris Kearns. *No Ordinary Time: Franklin & Eleanor Roosevelt: The Home Front in World War II*. New York: Simon & Schuster, Touchtone Books, 1994.

Halberstam, David. *The Fifties*. New York: Villard Books, 1993.

Janson, H. W. with Dora Jane Janson. *History of Art: A Survey of the Major Visual Arts from the Dawn of History to the Present Day*. Englewood Cliffs, N. J.: Prentice-Hall, Inc. and New York: Harry N. Abrams, Inc., 1966.

Karas, Sheryl. *The Solstice Evergreen: History, Folklore, and Origins of the Christmas Tree*. Boulder Creek, Cal.: Aslan Pub., 1991.

Larson, C. Kay. *'Til I Come Marching Home: A Brief History of American Women in World War II*. Pasadena, Md.: Minerva Press, 1995. Also see summary article at: www.nymas.org

_____. "North Star Rising: A History of Pleasure Boating in America, 1825-2000." Unpublished manuscript. Private papers.

Morris, Jeffrey B. and Richard B. Morris, ed. *Encyclopedia of American History*, 7th rev. ed. New York: HarperCollins Publishers, Inc., 1996.

Phillips, Kevin. *The Cousins' Wars: Religion, Politics & the Triumph of Anglo-America*. New York: Perseus Books Group, Basic Books, 1999.

Russiello, Nicholas A., as told to William D. Russiello. *GI in the Pacific War: Memoirs, 1941-1945*. Privately published: 2005.

Treuer, Robert. *The Tree Farm*. Boston: Little Brown, 1977.

Westervelt, Frances A. Johnson, ed. *History of Bergen County, New Jersey, 1630-1923*. New York: Lewis historical publishing co., 1923.

Van Valen, James M. *History of Bergen County, New Jersey*. New York: New Jersey publishing and engraving co., 1900.

Vardaman, James M. *Tree Farm Business Management*. New York: Ronald Press Co., 1965.

Government Documents

Ancestry.com: U. S. census database: sheet reprints, 1880-1930, New York Public Library.

Personal Interviews

Maine Evergreen Nursery, Inc., Maywood, New Jersey

Russell P. Trocano, president   Tony Dones
Guillermo Gutierrez   George Krayniak

Newspapers

America's Historical Newspapers, 1690-1922. Electronic database: New York Public Library. Articles accessed: tree farms/nurseries, 18th and 19th century advertisements.

National Newspapers. Electronic database: New York Public Library. Articles accessed on Bergen County, Hackensack and Maywood, N. J.

The New York Times, historical electronic database, New York Public Library. Articles accessed re: Hackensack and Maywood, N. J.; garden clubs; tree farm nurseries.

Websites

www.holland.nl/uk/holland/sights/tulips-history.html
www.nederlandstegelmuseum.nl/Museum/Geschiedenis_English.htm

ABOUT THE AUTHORS

C. Kay Larson, MBA, is a professional business writer and independent historian, specializing in report and technical writing and early American history. She is the author of *South Under a Prairie Sky: The Journal of Nell Churchill, US Army Nurse & Scout*; *Great Necessities: The Life, Times, and Writings of Anna Ella Carroll, 1815-1894*, on Abraham Lincoln's political/legal advisor; *'Til I Come Marching Home: A Brief History of American Women in World War II*. She also has published numerous articles, reviews, and internet material. Her business writings include a history of pleasure boating and technical projects conducted for New York City and State governments and engineering consultants.

Russell P. Trocano, Esq. is the great-grandson of Salvatore Costa, the founder of Costa Market, and grandson of Carmen and Edna Costa, founders of Maine Evergreen Nursery, Inc. Trocano is now the general manager of Maine Evergreen. He is also a practicing attorney in New Jersey and New York, specializing in general litigation. He heads the firm of Russell P. Trocano & Associates, located in Ridgewood, New Jersey.

About Maine Evergreen Nursery, Inc.

Maine Evergreen Nursery continues to be a prominent supplier of trees, shrubbery, and holiday greens, along with related supplies for northern New Jersey and the entire New York metropolitan region. Maine Evergreen looks forward to serving the needs of landscapers, garden centers, and floral customers, as it has for more than forty years.

Located at:

203 West Pleasant Avenue
Maywood, New Jersey 07607
Ph: 201-843-6808; F: 201-843-8845

𝓜𝒶𝒾𝓃𝑒 EVERGREEN
WHOLESALE NURSERY

> "You can't eat alone."
> — Carmen Costa (1913-1997), founder

Those were the watchwords of Carmen Costa, founder of Maine Evergreen Nursery, Inc, a family-owned, wholesale nursery business, located in Maywood, New Jersey. As revealed in the pages of this charming business history, Costa understood that true success must be shared. He built up his company by making sure that others besides him succeeded. The advice and help he gave workers, colleagues, and new contractors established a foundation for his own business. The people he helped over the years stayed on as workers and returned as customers. Meanwhile, Costa beautified New Jersey and the New York metropolitan region.

Mrs. Carmen Costa, Russell P. Trocano, the Costa and Trocano families, and the employees of Maine Evergreen Nursery, Inc. continue to proudly serve their customers, as they have since 1963.

$12.00
ISBN 978-0-578-00580-5
51200>

Maine Evergreen Nursery, Inc.
$12.00 - USA/Canada

9 780578 005805